HOW DOGE
AUDITING
IRS
IS FIRST
STEP TO
ABOLISHMENT
RANDALL SORENSEN CPA

How Doge Auditing IRS Is First Step to Abolishment

Library of Congress Control Number: 2025938063

About the Whistleblower

Randall C. Sorensen CPA CFF graduated from the University of North Dakota in 1979 and passed the Certified Public Accountant exam at age 22. He gained experience working for Fortune 500 companies before founding his own CPA practice in 1986. In 1995, he launched EZ DOC Corporation, a software company specializing in intellectual software for insurance companies and law firms.

His forensic experience at Coopers & Lybrand, CPA, caught the attention of Attorney Paul Eckstein, leading to his role as the key financial expert in Governor Evan Mecham's impeachment trial. By analyzing the governor's Pontiac dealership, Mr.

Sorensen justified his removal from office in just four hours. He received a commendation from the Arizona House of Representatives. To date, he has conducted over 2,000 forensic evaluations and testified on 85 occasions.

Beyond his accounting expertise, he has held licenses in insurance, real estate, and securities. He also served as President of the Arizona Chapter of the Forensic Expert Witness Association and the ASCPA Forensic Litigation Committee.

Representing himself *pro se* in the U.S. Tax Court, he challenged the IRS for allowing a national tax franchise to defraud the U.S. Treasury of $1.5 billion. The judge ruled that policing the IRS was not within his jurisdiction. Though the case was unwinnable due to the IRS's lack of transparency and disregard for the law, it fueled the ongoing debate over abolishing the agency.

Table of Contents

Chapter 1: DOGE Pulls Back Green Curtin

Elon Musk created controversy when he instructed DOGE to audit the Internal Revenue Service's records.

Pulling back the IRS's green curtain is extremely unflattering and could catapult it toward abolishment. Congress and taxpayers would witness corruption, fraud, abuse of power, security breaches, the targeting of older Americans, and cash giveaways to criminals and terrorists.

Randall Sorensen, CPA, CFF, has been practicing before the IRS for 40 years. He states, "The biggest problem with the IRS is that they have been accountable to no one."

The IRS claims to provide government transparency to Congress and the U.S. Treasury Inspector General for Tax Administration. TIGTA's audit will list 10 findings, and the IRS will pick and choose which ones they want to comply with. The fox has the keys to the hen house.

The horror stories shared among neighbors at backyard barbeques are only the tip of the iceberg. Listed below are IRS atrocities that would outrage the public if known.

The once highly respected and revered Internal Revenue Service has morphed into the largest legal **fraudulent** business in the United States. The IRS business model can be summed up in one word: “fear.” Nothing in life prepares a person for the genuine fear we experience when opening a letter from the IRS. It’s heart-stopping and one of the highest levels of pain we can self-impose.

This book will:

1. Reduce your fear of the IRS.
2. Detail how the IRS pays millions of people not to work (including employees).
3. Instruct you on how to protect yourself from tax refund theft.
4. Disclose disturbing news of the IRS handpicking Black individuals for prison.
5. Explain how Uncle Sam breached the identities of 170 million taxpayers.
6. Show how to stay two weeks ahead of the IRS.
7. Explain how the IRS missed two million tax frauds during the COVID-19 pandemic.

8. Provide examples of the IRS targeting older Americans.
9. Break down IRS trillion-dollar math errors.
10. Connect the dots to funding billions in weapons during the Iraq/Afghanistan wars.
11. Make a compelling argument for restructuring/ or abolishing the IRS.

Funding terrorists stings the most and by itself justifies **abolishing** the IRS. The fraud during the Great Recession wasn't exclusive to the U.S., as criminals worldwide were attracted to ***free*** money. These groups included such warm and fuzzy organizations as Al-Qaeda, Boko Haram, ISIS, and numerous other terrorist factions. Ultimately, antiquated technology and poor IRS leadership were responsible for funding terrorism.

The fear you feel toward the IRS is real and shared by **99%** of the population. One taxpayer became so distraught that he left a suicide note saying that the “IRS was bigger than him.” He apologized to his family for taking his life.

The next time you receive a notice from the IRS, I want you to envision yourself standing with Dorothy before the mighty ***Wizard of O***z. We’ve all seen the movie as kids and were temporarily stricken with paralysis due to panic and fear. It’s important to remember that after Dorothy’s dog, Toto, pulled back the green curtain, it exposed the terrifying Wizard of Oz for exactly what he was: a little old man putting on a disturbing show of power gone wrong.

The same is true for the IRS, which is credited with sending out 170 million notices of terror each year. Believe me when I say we all swallow a little harder and experience a rapid heartbeat when that letter arrives in the mail from the IRS.

It’s important to remember that 99% of these notices are computer-generated. No tax tiger is hiding, ready to devour you as its prey. The generic notice you receive will provide a 30-day window to send your response.

Remember to temper your fear of the IRS. Four of my tax clients received computer-generated notices demanding $550,000 in taxes, penalties, and interest. Upon closer review, the correct tax liability owed was $320. It's human nature to see an IRS letter in your mailbox and immediately think the worst. Here are the steps you need to follow:

The first step is to read each item the IRS proposes as an adjustment carefully. In many instances, the IRS taxes you a second time for income you've already reported. These errors are ***easily*** corrected by sending a letter to the IRS explaining the exact line item on Form 1040 where you previously reported the income. The issue will be resolved in six to twelve weeks.

Although factions of the IRS at times resemble Nazi stormtroopers, it's important to remember that there are some diamonds in the rough at the IRS. Sometimes, it comes down to the luck of the draw. If you're sensing hostility from the person on the other end of the phone, explain that you're at work and will have to call them back when it's more convenient. Getting another agent can be a game-changer.

The reason for my disdain for the IRS comes down to four reasons.

First, I alerted the IRS to three million tax frauds during the Great Recession and offered a solution to save hard-working Americans $15 billion. The IRS informed me they had no money to hire my company. Next, I offered to test 30 million tax returns in four hours for FREE. The IRS told me that Congress doesn't allow them to accept such offers. More pointedly, the IRS would have been trapped in its own lie to Congress, having previously testified that a tax fraud solution would be achieved.

Second, the AI technology I developed called Tax Return Score determined that a national tax franchise allowed clients to file fraudulent tax returns using "phantom income". For example, someone reports $18,800 for a non-existent cleaning business and qualifies for $9,200 in tax credits. No mops, dustpans or clients are required. I submitted my technology to the IRS Procurement Office and was contacted stating that my software was being considered at the highest levels of the IRS. Two months later, I received a letter indicating that the IRS already had a proto-type (mine) and due to tight resources, couldn't afford to pay me anyway.

Third, I identified a financial planner responsible for defrauding the U.S. Treasury of $20 million by failing to have his clients pay Social Security taxes on their earnings since 1984. A U.S. Tax Court judge ruled against me in favor of the IRS. The Judge said that only the IRS can determine tax fraud. Even more disturbing, he stated that he was not empowered to police the IRS. If a judge can't stop fraud committed by the IRS, who can?

Fourth, I delivered the IRS $400 million on a silver platter on behalf of you, the honest taxpayer. Commissioner Koskinen was guilty of malfeasance by failing to launch an investigation. Here is an individual who has made a career out of working for the federal government. By sticking around into his 70s, he was able to amass a triple pension. How many of us would like to receive $200K annually to support our golden years?

During his testimony to Congress, he was asked about his legal background. He smugly stated that he had “a cup of coffee” as an attorney and decided it wasn’t for him. He sounds like a kid who wasn’t picked to be on anyone’s team, so he took his ball and went home.

At the end of the book, I will make the case for phasing out the IRS by requiring only individuals making $100,001 or more to file. The IRS would compensate for lost revenue by implementing a 12% to 15% national sales tax.

Chapter 2: IRS Pays Millions of Folks Not to Work

Each year, between February 15th and March 31st, the IRS slices a **60-billion-dollar** money pie amongst 25 million **tax filers** (not to be confused with **taxpayers**). We have two groups of individuals who file tax returns: taxpayers and tax filers.

A taxpayer is your typical working stiff who gets up every morning, makes a laborious commute, and, at 5 o'clock, is free to head back to the comforts of their home. These individuals work from January 1st through April 24th just to satisfy their tax bill with Uncle Sam. They're the backbone of our country, and without them, the federal government would collapse. Things we take for granted—federal defense, entitlements, road infrastructure, and even research projects on the military viability of a Frisbee—would come to a screeching halt.

The second group files tax returns but doesn't actually pay income taxes. How does this work? Tax filers receive billions of dollars courtesy of taxpayers. Presidential candidate Mitt Romney famously referred to these individuals as the 47% who don't pay taxes. This one statement, said in jest, all but gift-wrapped the election for Barack Obama.

We'll refer to these individuals who don't pay taxes as "tax filers." I estimate they represent 75 million of the 160 million people who file income tax returns. Their dress attire is Friday casual—every day of the week. Sweatpants are a favorite, regardless of the fashion season. They don't have to worry about getting up at the crack of dawn to go to work because the IRS pays as many as 10 million folks to spend their day shopping at Walmart.

The story I'm about to tell you will outrage those who pay income taxes. The most common response will be, "How can this be true?" It's not only true but also one of the ugliest parts of the Internal Revenue Service.

Tax filers don't want taxpayers to know just how good a gig they have. If Congress ever decided to cut welfare out of the tax code, there would be a major revolt and riots in every major city across the U.S. I suspect one reason Congress allows as much as $100 billion in annual welfare fraud is that the cost of public upheaval would be prohibitive.

Black Friday shopping would cater to taxpayers instead of tax filers. Under the current tax entitlement system, tax filers happily spend $2,500 on Black Friday, knowing that the U.S. Treasury will be depositing a $5,000 refund in their bank account by March 1st. What started in 1975 as an admirable idea—expanded by Ronald Reagan to assist low-income parents—has morphed into a gigantic fraud that threatens the safety of all Americans, courtesy of the incompetency within the walls of the IRS.

How is the IRS defrauded? Jane Doe (mother of two) claims $18,800 in income from an imaginary cleaning business on her tax return. Since Jane doesn't have a business, she doesn't need to purchase any brooms, dustpans, cleaning supplies, or mops. For Jane's efforts, she qualifies for federal tax credits of $9,200. Before the U.S. Treasury deposits a $6,600 tax refund into her bank account, they also deposit $2,600 into her Social Security retirement account. From start to finish, Jane can complete her fraudulent tax return using phantom income in just 15 minutes!

Over 20 years, one dishonest taxpayer will defraud the U.S. Treasury of $300,000—without ever paying a dime in income taxes or working a day in their life.

Thirteen years ago, I submitted a proposal to the IRS that would eliminate this fraud. They literally tore apart the proposal (it was returned upside down) while expressing a high level of interest. Two months after kicking the tires, the IRS rejected my software, claiming they already had a prototype (untrue) and that they didn't have any money (another fable).

Thanks to congressional hearings regarding the targeting of tax-exempt entities, Congress confirmed that the IRS lied. In fact, at the same time the IRS said it didn't have money for cutting-edge technology, it entered into a $500 million software agreement with Strong Castle.

Clearly, a double standard exists within the top floors of the IRS. They severely punish taxpayers who slip up but fail miserably when IRS employees engage in deceit and fraud.

Due to severe IRS budget cuts, I offered to test 30 million tax returns for free. My rationale was that if I provided the IRS free usage of my software, they wouldn't be able to use the excuse of being broke.

They said they couldn't accept my offer for free and that I would need to submit a new application.

The IRS turned down $75 million in free technology that would have prevented $5 billion in tax fraud payments.

Chapter 3:
IRS Pays Employees Not to Work

Wouldn't you like a job that pays you $100,000 and qualifies you for an annual retirement of $70,000? Listed below is work the IRS took credit for but never conduct an investigation.

Phantom Investigation of $2 Billion Tax Fraud

In April 2010, a national tax franchise contacted me regarding software I had developed called Tax Return Score (TRS). TRS is an alternative method for evaluating an individual's creditworthiness, similar to a credit score. Using mathematical algorithms extracted from 160 million tax returns, the program measures taxpayer deviations and subtracts points to arrive at an overall letter grade.

The franchisor sought a solution to reduce the high loan loss ratio on holiday credit cards. The goal was to attract customers by giving them the buying power of their anticipated tax refunds for the upcoming season. However, their loss rate skyrocketed when folks either weren't eligible for a refund or never returned to have their taxes prepared.

The company agreed to send 2,000 tax returns for testing but instead sent 535,000. We tested the returns in two hours. In comparison, the IRS tested 550,000 returns over an entire year.

The testing revealed that 75% of the tax franchise's clients received either a D (Poor) or a U

(Unsatisfactory) for their tax scores. The bottom line? The majority of their clients were high-risk.

The company chose not to pursue a deal. However, our agreement encouraged the sharing of new ideas for technology.

As a result, the following year, I submitted a program called Earned Income Credit Compliance Audit (EICCA), which would alert tax preparers to potential fraud while the client was sitting across the table.

I informed the company's Board of Directors that this technology could prevent 640,000 of their clients from committing tax fraud.

I sent 46 letters urging them to stop the U.S. Treasury from losing $2 billion to fraud. However, the Board of Directors and senior management chose to do nothing—because stopping the fraud would have cost them $200 million in tax preparation revenue.

Due to their inaction, I blew the whistle on the national tax franchise for submitting 4,200 tax returns claiming phantom income to obtain $17 million in fraudulent refunds.

The fraudsters were easy to identify because they reported income in even $1,000 increments. The chance of 918 businesses all earning even amounts of gross income was 27 million to 1.

Exact Bus Income	Frequency	Exact Bus Income	Frequency
$3,000	80	**$9,000**	62
$4,000	65	**$10,000**	95
$5,000	72	**$11,000**	70
$6,000	79	**$12,000**	130
$7,000	63	**$13,000**	86
$6,000	48	**$14,000**	68

I received a letter from the IRS stating they had considered my whistleblower application, but the information did not result in the collection of any proceeds. They admitted to never investigating a single taxpayer out of 93,000 highly probable tax frauds!

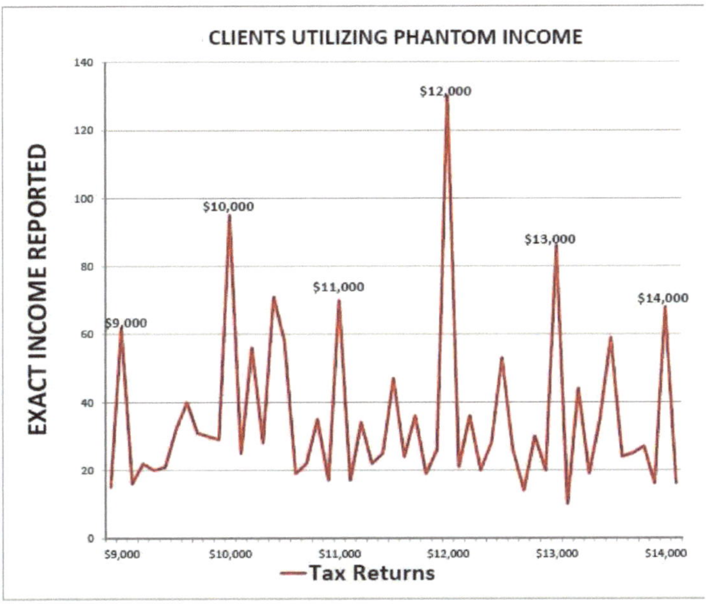

The IRS failed to perform its job and was equally responsible for the felonious activity. The IRS claimed they investigated the $2 billion fraud, but a Freedom of Information request verified that they had never bothered to investigate.

The second example of non-work involved a client's ex-husband. The former spouse had claimed the filing status of head of household for supporting his two daughters. The tax law required his daughters to live with him 183 days. The actual number of days was one. (I.e. Christmas Day)

The IRS again sent a letter indicating they "considered the information" but could not recover any tax proceeds. This was another instance of **fraud** by the IRS. They weren't aware that I was able to obtain internal documents four months later indicating that the IRS never conducted an investigation or even contacted the ex-husband. The IRS took credit for work never performed.

In the third fraud example, I turned in an individual I believed committed tax fraud while attending law school. The student had been advanced $75,000 to write a book, which meant he was an author and required to pay income and social security taxes.

The IRS sent a letter indicating they “considered the information” but could not recover any proceeds. The words “not able” would imply they did some work. The IRS took credit for investigating Barack Obama but never performed any work.

If the IRS were ever put on trial in Superior Court, the judge would charge them with perjury for failing to tell the truth, and the jurors would find them guilty of fraud.

Chapter 4:
75 IRS Staff & $170K to Defeat 1 CPA

I've endured some outlandish behavior from the IRS. For instance, I identified a tax fraud case that resulted in the IRS collecting $170,000. According to the Whistleblower Office, Congress limits them to paying a maximum reward of 10%, or $17,000. Not a fortune, but a tidy sum for a working stiff.

The IRS didn't see it that way, not even close. Instead, the IRS said I helped them collect $690 of the $170,000 and, therefore, was entitled to a reward of 10% or **$69.** However, since the IRS doesn't write checks for less than $100, they rounded my reward to **$0.** Nice work if you can get it…….or NOT!

I decided to appeal their decision to the U.S. Tax Court. Through document discovery I saw firsthand all of the emails and staff used to justify paying Randall Sorensen $0. Let's do the math:

Description	**Hourly Wages/Ben**	**IRS Spent**
75 IRS @ 3 Days	$95/hr	$170,000
Less: Savings Defrauding CPA		$17,000
Net Out-of-Pocket Cost		**$153,000**

There is something seriously wrong with this picture. I helped the IRS collect $170,000, and they spent $170,000 to ensure the whistleblower (aka Randall Sorensen) was paid $0. Had they not fought

Randall Sorensen, they would have enjoyed a windfall of $153,000. The IRS would have been money ahead by having the employees set up lemonade stands.

Chapter 5: IRS Handpicking Blacks for Prison

Listed below are 50 individuals whom the Department of Justice convicted for committing tax fraud. I believe the IRS is **guilty** of **targeting black** and Hispanic tax preparers while at the same time turning a **blind eye** to large tax companies who employ primarily white tax preparers:

Wiliesteina Jacobs
Detrick Tucker
Natashia Tucker
Keisha Stewart
Kavivah Bradley
Melissa Alvarez
Margaret Brown
Irene Smith
Greene Sheppard
Sabrina Lavant
Chandra Henderson
Rulon Sandoval
Acosta Hernandez
Carmen Martinez
Barbara Garrett
Noemi Baez
Sharon Rhodes
Joan Ledger
Lekesia Mills
Russ Burroughs
Latasha Failey
Kenya Hendrix
Chatonda Khofi
Ishmael Kosh
Amadou Sangaray
Francis Saygbay
Jessica Geddis
Grady Smith
John Hoang
Grady Smith
Stephanie Edmond
Joseph Burns
Joseph Thomas
Shawanda Nevrs
Hector Rangel
James Ericson
Markey Granberry
Derrick Robinson
Eumora Resse
Leslie Brewster
Saichelle McNeil
Cynthia Hawk
Stacy Middelton
George Cabrera
Clarence Barnes
Nataki Davis
Clarence Barnes
Oswaldo Diaz
Ann Williams
Jeffrey Applewhite

IRS Recommends Prosecution to DOJ

DEPARTMENT OF THE TREASURY
INTERNAL REVENUE SERVICE
WASHINGTON, D.C. 20224

Re Criminal Tax Violation

Dear: Mr.

A report recommending your client be prosecuted for evading Federal Income Taxes for the years 2013 through 2016 in violation of Title 26 States Code Section7201, was forwarded to Department of Justice Ta

(Figure 5.1 Source IRS)

Here are some facts that show the IRS would rather go after Black and Hispanic businesses—**easier prey**—than take on large corporations that can afford to spend millions on **attorneys** and **Washington lobbyists**:

Turbo Tax and H&R Block employ 100,000 tax preparers yet face few DOJ prosecutions.

The IRS Whistleblower Office refused to investigate a $2 billion tax fraud and ignored congressional inquiries from Senator Jon Kyl, Senator Jeff Flake, and Congressman Schweikart.

I was unwilling to accept this federal bureaucracy and filed a fraud complaint against the Whistleblower Office for failing to investigate a multi-billion-dollar tax fraud.

The **Department of Justice** refused to acknowledge my complaint. After eight months, I asked Senator Flake to intervene. Within days, the DOJ informed me that they **lacked jurisdiction** to investigate violations of federal tax laws.

How is it possible that the Department of Justice cannot enforce federal laws? The real irony is that the DOJ prosecuted more than 60 tax preparers in a single year—cases based on leads from the IRS. This means the **IRS Handpicks** tax preparers for prosecution, resulting in a DOJ conviction rate of 94%. Essentially, the fox instructs the farmer which chickens will be devoured from the henhouse that evening. The DOJ and IRS share equal shame in targeting Blacks and Hispanic tax preparers.

I think it's time to rename the Department of Justice to the Department of It Depends.

How has our judicial system warped into using unethical tactics to generate convictions?

Congress should be outraged that the DOJ is targeting Black tax preparers at the behest of the IRS.

In 1996, the U.S. Supreme Court ruled in *U.S. v. Armstrong* that racial profiling is constitutional in the absence of data proving that "similarly situated" defendants of another race were treated differently.

The ACLU should subpoena the IRS and demand all records regarding the **selection** and **convictions** of those on the list. Congress needs to identify **the criteria** used for recommending prosecution.

How would former IRS Commissioner John Koskinen feel if he were handpicked for DOJ prosecution by taxpayers affiliated with Black Lives Matter?

The **corrupt** and **deceptive** tactics used by Lois Lerner to target Tea Party members permeate throughout the IRS.

If our country is serious about improving all aspects of social justice, then I believe it's time to **abolish** the IRS—for racism and for defrauding the American public.

Chapter 6: Uncle Sam Breached Identities of 170 Million

The mortgage industry played a principal role in the 2008 real estate crash that jump-started the Great Recession.

In 2007, while attending a mortgage convention in Las Vegas, one of the guest speakers asked attendees from all 50 states whether anyone had a mortgage loan that hadn't received approval in the last year. This question sparked an outburst of belly laughs from the attendees. Not one person out of 2,000 raised their hand. If these same people had known the mortgage business was about to collapse, they wouldn't have laughed.

In the fall of 2006, I sent a letter to the Federal Housing Administration explaining the benefits of dissecting the tax returns of loan applicants. I proposed **verifying** the loan applicant's stated income directly with the Internal Revenue Service. What a bizarre concept.... I wanted to check to determine whether a loan applicant was ***actually earning*** the income they had scribbled down on a mortgage application.

I was quickly informed that any changes to policies that had been in place since the 1970s would require an act of Congress. No one listened, and in December 2007, we entered a temporary purgatory called the Great Recession.

By 2006, I was already a 20-year veteran as a financial forensic expert. Back in 1988, I had served as the forensic accountant in the impeachment trial of Arizona Governor Evan Mecham. He famously referred to Black Americans as "piccaninnies," and even though I was a registered Republican at the time, I knew he needed to be removed from office ASAP. The Governor had accumulated his wealth from his Pontiac car dealership. He had gotten into a jam by loaning $80,000 from his political campaign fund to his Pontiac dealership. Governor Mecham testified that rather than letting the money sit around, it could be drawing interest from his business. I determined the Governor was playing with fire over $9 a day in interest income.

On my first day on the job, I prepared an analysis of the dealership's cash flow, which showed that the Pontiac dealership would have been **$70,000 in the red** if not for the campaign loan. The attorneys prosecuting the Governor were jumping for joy—they now had their **smoking gun**. Before Mecham was removed from office, I escaped to Minneapolis as a precautionary safety measure. How ironic that 32 years later, Minneapolis wouldn't have been an option for peace and tranquility.

I received my 15 minutes of fame, making national TV and front-page headlines in newspapers from coast to coast.

From that brief stint in the limelight, I parlayed a 35-year career as a forensic expert witness.

During that time, I saw individuals using two sets of tax returns to defraud insurance companies. In one Allstate claim, a claimant submitted a bogus tax return to the insurance company while reporting 50% less income to the IRS. That was the first time I realized the power of tax fraud—and how much the American public, as jurors, doesn't tolerate it.

Because of mandated court deadlines, I needed a way to obtain tax records faster than the 10–20 business days I was waiting for. The IRS came up with a solution.

In 2006, they created IVES—Income Verification Express Service. Here's how it works: a loan applicant Signs IRS Form 4506-T, allowing a third party to obtain copies of their tax records within 24–48 hours.

There was also some money involved. By charging $5 per transcript, the IRS created its own personal ATM machine, generating upwards of $100 million.

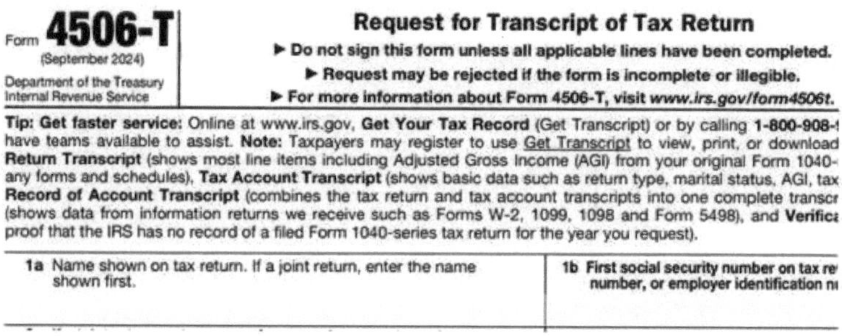

Form **4506-T**
(September 2024)
Department of the Treasury
Internal Revenue Service

Request for Transcript of Tax Return
▶ Do not sign this form unless all applicable lines have been completed.
▶ Request may be rejected if the form is incomplete or illegible.
▶ For more information about Form 4506-T, visit *www.irs.gov/form4506t*.

Tip: Get faster service: Online at www.irs.gov, **Get Your Tax Record** (Get Transcript) or by calling **1-800-908-** have teams available to assist. **Note:** Taxpayers may register to use Get Transcript to view, print, or download **Return Transcript** (shows most line items including Adjusted Gross Income (AGI) from your original Form 1040- any forms and schedules), **Tax Account Transcript** (shows basic data such as return type, marital status, AGI, tax **Record of Account Transcript** (combines the tax return and tax account transcripts into one complete transcr (shows data from information returns we receive such as Forms W-2, 1099, 1098 and Form 5498), and **Verifica** proof that the IRS has no record of a filed Form 1040-series tax return for the year you request).

1a Name shown on tax return. If a joint return, enter the name shown first.

1b First social security number on tax re number, or employer identification n

(Figure 10.1 Form 4506-T)

I entered the tax transcript business to cash in on this technology. I quickly discovered that I was a small fish in a massive pond. A few large companies had gotten in on the ground floor ten years earlier and were now processing thousands of tax transcripts daily—making millions. This was one of the first instances of corruption I witnessed within the walls of the IRS. Deals had been cut behind closed doors, giving certain companies advantages the rest of the public wasn't privy to.

What started as the IRS throwing a big, juicy bone to mortgage lenders has morphed into a massive fraud scheme— one that compromises personal identities and poses a direct threat to the safety of every American by providing criminals with **free money.**

And what about the carnage caused by the weapons purchased by terrorists? Twenty-two thousand U.S. casualties resulted from improvised explosive devices (IEDs).

The table below shows that the IRS processed an additional 55 million tax transcripts and delivered them to third parties with minimal or no security vetting for fraud. It also includes home sales and estimated identity breaches caused by the IRS. When factoring in spouses and children, the total rises to 110 million.

F/Y	4506-T's Processed	Homes Sold	Ratio	Expected 4506-T's	Possible Breaches
9/10	21,400,000	4.2 mil	5.1	(7.4 mil)	14.0 mil
9/11	23,100,000	4.3 mil	5.4	(7.6 mil)	15.5 mil
9/12	19,100,000	4.7 mil	4.1	(8.3 mil)	10.8 mil
9/13	24,000,000	5.1 mil	4.7	(9.0 mil)	15.0 mil
	87,600,000			**(32.3 mil)**	**55.3 mil**
Plus	Spouses & Children Identities				**2X**
Total Identities Compromised by IRS					**110.6 mil**

Earlier, I mentioned my foray into the tax transcript business. Instead of processing thousands of orders daily, we were handling only a handful—except for the night of February 29, 2012. That night, my phone was blowing up with email notifications of 4506-T transcript requests.

In just four hours, the cybercriminals had submitted 50 requests, all from three families: Craxx, Robxxxxx, and Stexxx. For a brief moment, I was thrilled with the surge in business.

But before celebrating, I decided to do my own due diligence. One common detail among the tax release forms was that every transcript request used an email account ending in @inbox.com. Curious, I visited the website to see what Inbox.com was all about.

Inbox.com provided visitors with a "free" email account—on the condition that they install its browser on their computer, a method that allows the company to embed cookies and monitor every move the user made.

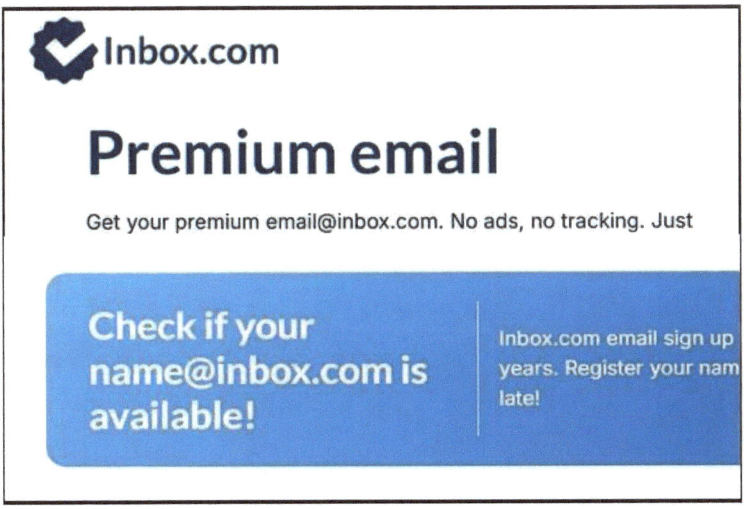

The bizarre part was that you could search for names to see if an email address was in service. I typed in Randall.Sorensen@inbox.com to check if I was at risk of identity theft. Luckily, the name was not in use.

Even though I had been a software developer for over 15 years, I never, in my wildest dreams, imagined someone stealing my identity by using a bogus email account. I recommend you check and vet that site.

I did some additional due diligence and discovered that cybercriminals had breached the firewalls of credit unions in Minneapolis and Chicago. Next, I sent an SOS to the IRS, reporting that I had uncovered a major breach that I believed was widespread nationwide. Here is the exact text:

"I wanted to send your IVES Team a fraud alert. Earlier today we identified an individual who apparently has stolen the identity of numerous individuals. Your IVES Team won't be able to detect

the fraud on your end. However, the tax fraud is using the following email addresses:

Example: John.Doe@inbox.com

Example: Jane.Doe@inbox.com

I would encourage all IVES participants to be vigilant and heavily scrutinize any new customers using inbox.com. The identity theft fraud is utilizing home addresses from St. Paul and Chicago. If you have any questions, please don't hesitate to give me a call."

I waited for a response that never materialized. I informed a friend, and he began a covert operation to discover why the IRS had failed to respond to my fraud SOS.

He confirmed that the IRS had never investigated the potentially massive fraud that was, at a minimum, cutting a wide swath through our country's heartland.

This was yet another example of how the IRS defrauded taxpayers by failing to protect us from cybercriminals, using the flippant excuse of having no money. Even more disturbing was a national conference call on June 12, 2015, between the IRS and IVES participants. During the call, I asked Robert Shearer why the IRS had finally taken action more than three years after being informed of a massive fraud.

I stated that the over/under on identity breaches was five million. The moderator on the conference call fell silent. After a long pause, he finally asked if I could provide him with a copy of the email that had been sent to him and four others in 2012.

One thing I've learned about the IRS is that they are far more often wrong than right. Although TIGTA (Taxpayer Inspector General for Tax Administration) attempts to hold the IRS accountable by writing scathing reports on ineptitude, they do nothing if the IRS disagrees with a documented deficiency.

Imagine your boss telling you that your daily tardiness is unacceptable. Instead of agreeing to show up on time, you simply inform your boss that you disagree with their assessment. That, in a nutshell, is why the IRS is the largest legal fraudulent entity operating in the U.S.—no accountability!

I sprang into action once I realized the IRS planned to bury its head in the sand. If they didn't care about these people, I sure did. I felt deep empathy for these taxpayers whom the Internal Revenue Service had unceremoniously tossed aside. Even worse than potentially destroying people's identities was that the IRS pretended not to know.

I began drafting and mailing letters to every affected individual. I thought I might receive a phone call thanking me for the heads-up on cybercrime. Instead, one of the very people I was trying to help turned me into the Minnesota Attorney General's Office.

I was shocked when I received a phone call from the AG's office that was anything but cordial. I spent

20 minutes defending myself against pointed questions as if they were trying to get me to confess to something.

I wasn't about to take the bait and admit to a crime I hadn't committed. Instead, I fielded their questions and convinced the Minnesota Attorney General's Office that I was simply trying to help. The old saying *no good deed goes unpunished* was certainly in play.

Another way the Internal Revenue Service is guilty of breaching taxpayers' identities is through federal tax liens recorded by the local recorder.

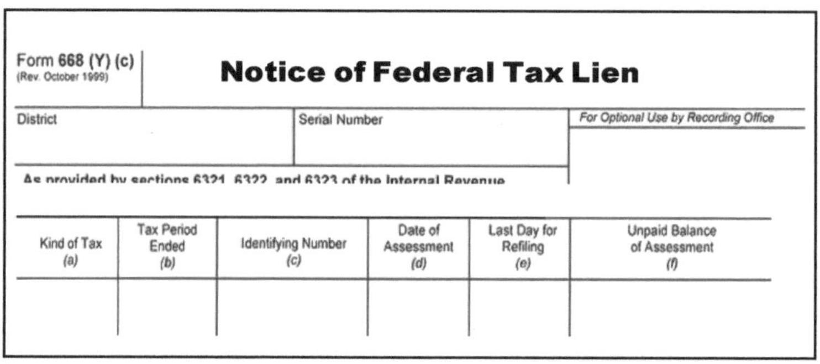
Form 668 (Y) (c)
(Rev. October 1999)

Notice of Federal Tax Lien

District | Serial Number | For Optional Use by Recording Office

As provided by sections 6321, 6322, and 6323 of the Internal Revenue

Kind of Tax (a)	Tax Period Ended (b)	Identifying Number (c)	Date of Assessment (d)	Last Day for Refiling (e)	Unpaid Balance of Assessment (f)

(Figure 10.2 Form 668)

If you don't pay your taxes in full when you file your tax return, you'll receive a bill usually within 60 days. The IRS can file a federal tax claim against the property you own.

This includes seizing wages, bank accounts, social security benefits, and retirement income. The IRS may also seize your auto and recreational vehicles and sell real estate to settle your unpaid tax debt.

The top of the next page lists the federal liens filed and an estimate for the last twenty years.

Year	Federal Tax Liens
2008	970,000
2009	1,100,000
2010	1,000,000
2011	710,000
2012	600,000
2013	540,000
2014	520,000
2015	470,000
2016	450,000
Avg	710,000
Years: 2004 thru 2023	x 20
Exposed So. Sec. No.'s	**14,200,000**

(Figure 10.3 Bankruptcy Voluntary Petition)

On the surface, it's no big deal to most folks because financial institutions have used the last four digits of our Social Security numbers for years. I still remember proudly ordering my first check blanks and requesting my Social Security number to be printed right below my name and address. Back in the 1970s, it was common practice, and the internet was still twenty years away.

I set out to determine if I could compromise the identity of my uncle, mother, sister, and myself. The first thing I discovered was that North Dakota has only two prefixes for Social Security numbers: 501 and 502. The 502 prefix has been used exclusively since the late 1940s. So now I had the first three and the last four digits—leaving only the middle two. However, that wasn't a big deal since only 99 possible combinations exist. Cybercriminals could easily identify the correct combination using computer software in less than a microsecond.

Thinking I had cracked the ability to compromise my relative's Social Security numbers, I began researching online. I found an article discussing Social Security numbers and reached out to the author. He informed me that I could simply sign up for investigative searches with Westlaw.

I contacted them, and they provided a sample of their technology. I selected an individual who had defrauded my mother of $300,000. Westlaw provided a report that was 100 pages long, detailing employment history, addresses, social networks, properties, bankruptcies, and criminal charges. What a great way to vet a potential employee, business partner, or spouse. The crown jewel of the report was the first five digits of the person's Social Security number.

Let's do a quick recap. So far, the IRS has compromised 110.6 million Social Security numbers through the IVES program and an additional 14.2 million via federal tax liens—for a combined total of 124.8 million. The third component of Uncle Sam's breach of taxpayer identities is through the U.S. Bankruptcy Court. Specifically, the bankruptcy petition requires debtors to disclose the last four digits of their Social Security number.

(Official Form 1) (12/03)

FORM B1 **United States Bankruptcy Court District of Arizona**	**Voluntary Petition**
Name of Debtor (if individual, enter Last, First, Middle): **WOODCOCK, DARYL**	Name of Joint Debtor (Spouse)(Last, First, Middle):
All Other Names used by the Debtor in the last 6 years (include married, maiden, and trade names):	All Other Names used by the Joint Debtor in the last 6 years (include married, maiden, and trade names):
Last four digits of Soc. Sec. No. / Complete EIN or other Tax I.D. No. (if more than one, state all): **XXX-XX-6515**	Last four digits of Soc. Sec. No. / Complete EIN or other Tax I.D. N more than one, state all):
Street Address of Debtor (No. & Street, City, State & Zip Code): **8723 E. NATAL CIRCLE MESA, AZ. 85206**	Street Address of Joint Debtor (No. & Street, City, State & Zip Cod
County of Residence or of the Principal Place of Business: **MARICOPA**	County of Residence or of the Principal Place of Business:

(Figure 6.3 Bankruptcy Voluntary Petition)

I performed research on individual and corporate bankruptcies. Both groups proved to be equally toxic when it came to disclosing personal information that criminals could feast on. Corporate bankruptcies disclose the last four of the shareholders' social security numbers. In closely held corporations, this would include both the husband and wife.

Listed below is a recap of bankruptcy filings every 5th year since 1985.

Year		Bankruptcies
1985		500,000
1990		750,000
1995		1,000,000
2000		1,250,000
2005		2,000,000
2010		1,500,000
2015		750,000
Avg		1,100,000
Years: 1980 thru 2017		38
Exposed So. Sec. No.'s		41,800,000
Plus: Spouse So. Sec #	44%	18,400,000
Subtotal		60,200,000
Less: Mortality	-25%	(15,100,000)
Est. Compromised Identities		**45,100,000**

(Figure 10.4 Bankruptcy Identities)

When you take the 124.8 million compromised identities from IVES and federal tax liens and add 45.1 million, you arrive at a grand total of **170 million** breached identities.

Chapter 7: How to Stay Ahead of IRS Moves

I'm willing to bet a close acquaintance has poured their heart to you regarding their IRS problems over a glass of wine or a beer in the backyard.

I will share a little secret that I stumbled across 10 years ago while assisting a friend who hadn't filed taxes in 14 years. The IRS has a service called Get Transcript Online.

You can access this service by visiting irs.gov. To register you will need:

- Social Security number
- date of birth
- filing status
- mailing address from latest return
- an email account
- your personal account number, a credit card, or mortgage
- a mobile phone with your name on the account

Next, you can choose from the following tax data: 1) tax return transcripts, 2) account transcripts, 3) record of account transcripts or 4) wage & income transcripts.

Request the wage and income transcripts for filing delinquent tax returns. If you need to go back more than four years, you can submit multiple 4506-T. I've obtained records from 20 years ago.

The way to learn what the IRS has in store is to request an account transcript. The account transcript will confirm that you haven't filed, list federal tax payments you've made, and, most importantly, show any notices the IRS is planning to send.

In my friend's case, the account transcript indicated the IRS was mailing an inquiry about not filing five days from now. As a result, we sent the returns overnight to beat the IRS by four days.

Depending on where you live, I strongly recommend verifying their address for overnight deliveries. Start by doing an address search on irs.gov.

The goal is to get your returns filed before the IRS gets you.

Chapter 8: How Web, IRS & $60 Can Ruin Your Life

If you're like millions of Americans, you've received a notification from American Express, Equifax, Facebook, Home Depot, Target, or a plethora of other retailers indicating a possible breach of your personal information. I've received one from all of the above companies.

Identity theft notices have become mainstream and no longer instill fear in us like the first one did.

Five years ago, I came across a website offering personal information on people. The one I use is called Instant Checkmate. The service assists a single woman or man in vetting a prospective date or marriage candidate.

Since then, I've conducted over 500 searches, including inquiries on parents, siblings, friends, classmates, girlfriends, clients, or anyone I wanted information on.

The game changer was finding a website that offered similar services with one exception: You could request a person's Social Security number.

I was curious but didn't want to break the law. As a test, I requested my mother's Social Security number while watching TV. To my astonishment, I received a notification that my order was completed by 10:00 the next morning.

The information regarding my mother was spot on. For my second test, I submitted my own name. My order was rejected because it was illegal for me to obtain my own Social Security number.

Let that sink in for a minute. I could obtain the Social Security number of any one of 350 million Americans, but it was deemed illegal to obtain my own. The service costs $50.

I guess now I've got your full attention. A Social Security number is a good start, but it's not enough. In addition to the Social Security number, you need the person's income as reported on their taxes.

Again, I turned to the internet and found a service that, for $10, allowed me to obtain four years of tax return records and one year of employment information. That's **game**, set, and **match**.

A cybercriminal is now empowered to:

Steal your tax refund

Obtain your credit report, including all account numbers

Open credit cards

Buy a car

Apply for a mortgage

Fly to Vegas and max out every one of your credit cards

Don't be fooled into thinking that once you alert your financial institution, you'll only be out $50.

According to the Identity Theft Resource Center, they reported the following:

- 75% of victims were severely distressed
- 61% hadn't cleared credit 5 years later
- 26% of respondents had to borrow money
- 25% sought professional counseling
- 22% took time off work

Most individuals said they discovered their breach within three months, but 16% didn't find out for three years. Out-of-pocket losses ranged from $600 to $6,000.

Data Breach Growth

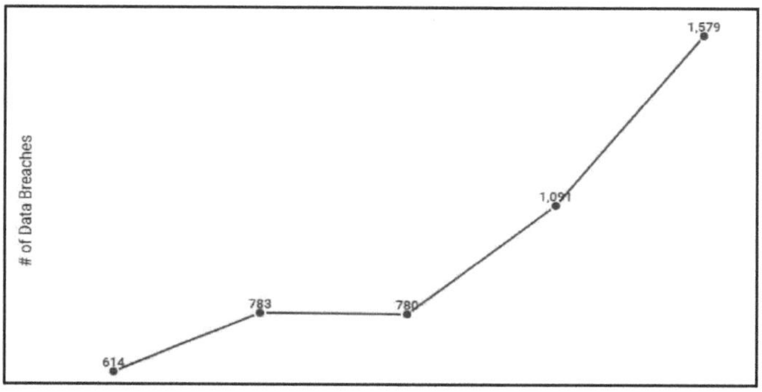

There are companies like LifeLock that you can sign up with to be alerted of attempts to use your credit.

Ironically, the IRS provides the best means to prevent a cybercriminal from stealing your tax refund: the **Affidavit of Identity Theft** (IRS Form 14039).

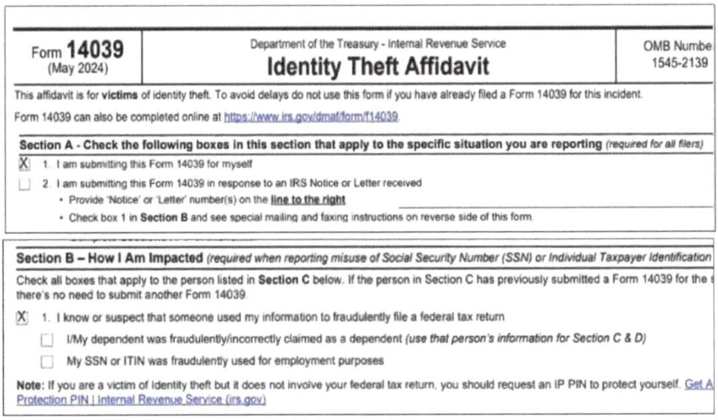

Form **14039** (May 2024) | Department of the Treasury - Internal Revenue Service | **Identity Theft Affidavit** | OMB Numbe 1545-2139

This affidavit is for **victims** of identity theft. To avoid delays do not use this form if you have already filed a Form 14039 for this incident.

Form 14039 can also be completed online at https://www.irs.gov/dmaf/form/f14039.

Section A - Check the following boxes in this section that apply to the specific situation you are reporting *(required for all filers)*

[X] 1. I am submitting this Form 14039 for myself

[ ] 2. I am submitting this Form 14039 in response to an IRS Notice or Letter received

- Provide 'Notice' or 'Letter' number(s) on the **line to the right**
- Check box 1 in **Section B** and see special mailing and faxing instructions on reverse side of this form.

Section B – How I Am Impacted *(required when reporting misuse of Social Security Number (SSN) or Individual Taxpayer Identification*

Check all boxes that apply to the person listed in **Section C** below. If the person in Section C has previously submitted a Form 14039 for the
there's no need to submit another Form 14039.

[X] 1. I know or suspect that someone used my information to fraudulently file a federal tax return

[ ] I/My dependent was fraudulently/incorrectly claimed as a dependent *(use that person's information for Section C & D)*

[ ] My SSN or ITIN was fraudulently used for employment purposes

Note: If you are a victim of identity theft but it does not involve your federal tax return, you should request an IP PIN to protect yourself. Get A
Protection PIN | Internal Revenue Service (irs.gov)

The form doesn't require that you have already been a victim. If you suspect that your identity has been compromised (a high probability for the entire population), you can file Form 14039. For the reason for filing, I stated:

"I was contacted by a major credit bureau and Home Depot that my personal information had been compromised."

Department of the Treasury
Internal Revenue Service
Fresno, CA 93888-0025

Notice	CP01C
Notice date	March 12, 2018
To contact us	1-800-908-4490
Your Caller ID	356241
Page 1 of 2	29H

150185.688338.161822.9366 1 AB 0.408 373

RANDALL C SORENSEN

Message about your identity theft documents

We verified your documents to support your identity theft report

We verified your documents and marked your account with an identity theft indicator. Identity theft is a serious issue and we're committed to helping taxpayers who are affected by it.

What you need to do

- Continue to file all federal tax returns.
- If you have a balance owed, continue sending your payments.

Next Steps:

- You have the opportunity to create an online account at irs.gov/dataippin
- An Identity Protection PIN is a six-digit number used on a paper or electronically filed return that helps verify your identity and prevents misuse of your social security number

- If you choose to receive an IP PIN, you will receive a new IP PIN in the mail each December/January for the upcoming filing season.

I was extremely skeptical before I faxed my request for protection. It's the best return on investment you'll ever receive for 10 minutes of your time.

The process is seamless, and the protection is outstanding. Mail the completed form to:

Department of the Treasury
Internal Revenue Service Fresno,
CA 93888-0025

If you checked Box 2 in Section B of Form 14039 (non-tax-related issue), then fax the form to: 855-807-5720

For a fillable form and instructions, visit irs.gov, click "Forms," and enter 14039.

Chapter 9: IRS Extortion and So. Sec. # Breach

The IRS attempted to extort $550,000 from my tax clients and stole a much-deserved $17,000 reward from my hands.

The next story should alarm every person living in the United States. In an earlier chapter I mentioned that I turned in a tax fraud that resulted in a $170,000 windfall for the Internal Revenue Service. If you ever decide to turn someone in for tax fraud you'll need to file form 211 to identify the alleged perpetrator to claim your reward.

On February 13th, 2017, I submitted form 211 to identify a $170,000 fraud. The Whistleblower Office then sent a notification letter dated March 6th, 2017. Does anything strike you odd in the address below? Well, the IRS used my social security number for my zip code!

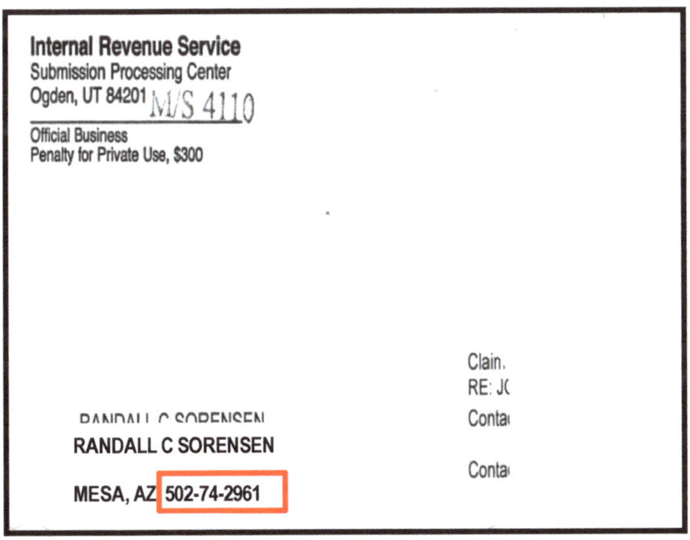

Internal Revenue Service
Submission Processing Center
Ogden, UT 84201 M/S 4110

Official Business
Penalty for Private Use, $300

Clain.
RE: J(
Conta
Conta

RANDALL C SORENSEN
MESA, AZ 502-74-2961

(Figure 13.1 IRS Letter)

As a result, the letter wasn't delivered until May 12th, 2017. It just so happens that the first five letters of my social security number are exactly the same as Wiota, Iowa. I can only speculate, but it would seem very likely that my letter bounced around post offices between Iowa and Arizona before showing up in my mailbox 60 days later.

I decided to do a deeper dive and sent a letter to Whistleblower Office Director Lee Martin requesting an investigation. One year later, I was able to confirm that their "investigation" consisted of issuing Randall Sorensen an apology. They never made an effort to get to the truth.

Identity stats show that if the IRS breaches my identity, I will suffer a financial loss of up to $30,000, and it will take 600 hours to fix the damage done by the IRS.

I asked a friend who is a forensic computer expert if putting my social security number on my letter could have been an accident. He answered that it had to be intentional.

So, my good deed of delivering a gift of $170,000 not only resulted in me being paid nothing, but I may fork out $30,000 in identity theft costs because of helping the IRS. Never again!

Chapter 10: Threatening 5 Years Prison Just for Asking

Here are examples of IRS power gone wrong. Several years ago, I paid a $16 invoice from the IRS four days late. The IRS reacted swiftly with a letter:

- Charging an effective interest rate of **11,400%**
- Notifying intent to initiate salary and/or admin offset to recover the debt
- Indicating intention to initiate a tax refund offset

- Stating right to request a hearing w/ impartial judge
- Giving the option to agree to a written agreement

> This will also serve as your notice to initiate salary and/or administrative offset to recover debt, including accumulated interest, penalty and administrative offset (30) days after the date of receipt of this notice. We will also initiate tax refund offset, if applicable, sixty (60) days after the date of receipt of this notice. You have certain rights prior to initiating offset procedures. Your rights are as follows:
>
> Salary Offset (Current IRS Employees Only) - We will offset your periodic salary payments no more than fifteen (15) percent of your disposable pay beginning with the first salary payment thirty (30) days after the date of receipt of this notice. You have the right to request a hearing by an impartial official with respect to the existence and amount of the debt or proposed offset schedule.

Another instance of IRS power gone wrong occurred in September of 2019. Two months prior, President Trump had signed the Taxpayer First Act. It said the Secretary can disclose return information related to the investigation of any taxpayer with respect to whom the individual (Randall Sorensen) has provided such information with respect to the correct determination of tax liability.

As a result, I requested the following records:

Administrative file

1. Tax transcripts obtained by the IRS
2. Tax examination work papers

I wanted to confirm that the IRS worked on some projects and identified the official responsible for rejecting and declining my offer to test 25 million tax returns for ***free.***

Instead of thanking me for identifying one of the largest fraud cases in the history of the United States, the IRS **threatened me with 5 years of imprisonment** if I disclosed the information below:

Dear Randall C. Sorensen, CPA

We are responding to your request for information on the status and stage of your claim referenced above. Internal Revenue Code (IRS) section 6103(k)(13) requires that the Whistleblower Office provide this notice to you. Your claim is currently in the Litigation Stage.

The Litigation Stage includes the claims where the whistleblower has brought litigation regarding an award determination made on the whistleblower's claim.

We are unable to provide additional information at this time. It is important to understand that it could take several years until a determination can be reached on this claim.

Disclosure of the information contained in this letter to any person, except as authorized by USC Title 26, may be a felony punishable by a fine in an amount not exceeding $5,000 or imprisonment of not more than 5 years, or both, together with the costs of prosecution under IRC.

How can an IRS veteran with three years of experience and no CPA threaten prison for asking for information promised by law?

Congress should hold IRS employees accountable through formal investigations and, where appropriate, legal proceedings for misconduct against taxpayers. This includes allegations of harassment, mental abuse, wrongful asset seizure, and the infliction of undue economic hardship.

The most recent example of unchecked power was committed in November 2019 by an attorney for the Commissioner of the Internal Revenue Service. The unscrupulous lawyer fabricated records and committed perjury nearly a dozen times.

The US Tax Court mandates a response to the Request for Production of Documents in 30 days. This particular attorney wanted to comply with a deadline and called one Friday afternoon while I enjoyed happy hour with friends. She hung up the first time that I answered. On the second call, two minutes later, I sent the call directly to voice mail. Her voice conveyed her nervousness while she left a rambling and confused message.

She claimed she had sent a UPS package the day before to comply with a court deadline. She indicated that I should have already received the package. Why would the attorney need to tell me to expect a package that I had already received?

This sequence of events reminds me of the movie *A Few Good Men.* In a pivotal scene, Lt. Daniel Kaffee (played by Tom Cruise) questions Colonial Nathan Jessup (played by Jack Nicholson) why Private Santiago needed to be transferred if Jessup had ordered that Santiago not be harmed. Under intense pressure, an enraged Colonel Jessup suffers a meltdown and admits to ordering the "code red."

I decided to do some fact-checking and called UPS.

I was informed that there had never been a package. If Private Santiago was flying out the next morning, why hadn't he packed?

When I confronted the attorney, she knew her story was dead in the water. This would've been grounds for the State Bar Association to sanction her with a suspension to practice law.

She wiggled her way out by saying that it would be against the law for her to provide me with a copy of the alleged UPS air bill. Yet the document had my name on it, and it certainly wasn't me she was trying to protect. She had a get-out-of-jail card and played it.

She committed perjury when she said the package had been delivered to another taxpayer. She was so concerned that she had given away my identity that she never bothered to contact UPS to ask for a redelivery.

Rather than immediately correct her mistake she did nothing to protect my personal information that she was responsible for sending to a complete stranger.

Pulling back the green curtain exposed a federal employee for exactly what she was a fraud.

It's crystal clear that the IRS relishes putting the fear of God into people with the threat of fines and imprisonment. Even worse is a federal judge admitting that it's not his job to "**police the IRS**."

The coup de gras is an attorney who is sworn to uphold the law and instead obliterates the truth. The same laws used to convict honest people allow IRS employees immunity from prosecution.

The IRS inflicts as much pain as any bad cop. Public videos do provide some accountability. In contrast, the IRS wields a stick of ill-gotten power that terrorizes and ruins lives. The public never gets to witness firsthand the carnage of the IRS.

I propose body cameras that record selfies of IRS employees when interacting with taxpayers.

Justice provided for unjust actions.

Chapter 11: IRS Targeting Older Americans

The man in the photo is Eric Henshall, who graced the cover of Look magazine during the Vietnam War. Eric was born in Scotland and brought to the United States by his recently widowed mother. Eric's father had been killed in WWII before he was born.

Eric enlisted and served in the Army, and after his discharge, he enlisted in the Marines. Eric was trained as a sniper and had 40 confirmed kills.

Eric sometimes went for weeks without showering because the scent of soap could give off his position to the NVA or Viet Cong.

Eric was a highly decorated war hero. He received three purple hearts and a bronze star and spent six months in a military hospital due to his combat wounds. Eric was deemed fully disabled upon discharge and lives off his disability income.

Eric suffered elderly abuse by the IRS when he received a tax notice demanding $11,000 during the pandemic. The IRS falsely accused Eric of receiving social security benefits totaling $251,000 when his SSA-1099 listed $21,000.

FARMINCOMEORLOSS(SCHEDULEF):	$0.00
FARM INCOME OR LOSS (Schedule F) PER COMPUTER:	$0.00
UNEMPLOYMENT COMPENSATION:	$0.00
TOTAL SOCIAL SECURITY BENEFITS:	**$251,030.00**

I ran into Eric, and he was stressed. He told me that he hadn't slept in two months because the IRS letter demanded $11,000. The IRS had passed judgment on Eric without even hearing from him.

This is mind-boggling since the largest retirement possible was $50,000. This was not just a mistake; it was a nightmare. The IRS failed to cross-check the correct data with the Social Security Administration.

I contacted the IRS and explained that the IRS had made a huge mistake. After an hour on the phone, the IRS acknowledged the error and corrected their horrific error.

Eric will turn 82 years old this November. How healthy is it for any person to be on pins and needles for months?

What if Eric had suffered a stroke or became distraught and harmed himself courtesy of the IRS harassment?

How many seniors are targeted by the Internal Revenue Service strictly because it's easy money?

Margie Rammer, an 84-year-old grandmother, was informed by the IRS that she withdrew $150,000 from taxable retirement income, deducted medical expenses of $78,000, and had federal taxes withheld of $22,500.

Margie had been the victim of identity theft, and the thieves stole $7,500 from the US Treasury. The IRS never informed Margie about the fraud.

She only found out when she received a Christmas letter from SSA indicating that because she reported an income of $150,000, her Medicare

Part B premium was increasing by $4,000 in 2021. The IRS never bothered to cross-check the data.

Here is what was really disturbing. The IRS allowed the fraudster to file "single" even though Margie had been married for 65 years.

When I performed a closer review, I determined that the IRS has a default setting of single. Basically, the IRS assumes everyone is single even though there are 90 million married folks in the United States.

In hockey terms, the Internal Revenue Service security system is a complete sieve. The largest free ATM and open to the world.

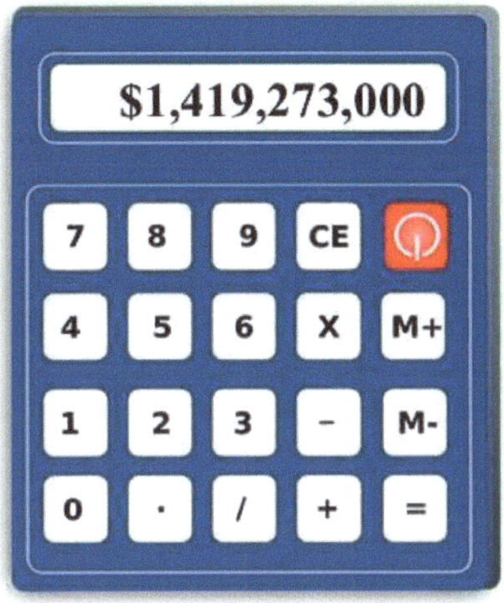

Chapter 12: IRS Math Errors Totaling $1.4 Trillion

If your tax accountant made math errors on 97% of their tax calculations, would you have any confidence in their abilities? If your physician made errors on 97% of their diagnosis, would you keep them?

Would you be surprised that the IRS can't do fifth-grade math? I audited tax statistics for 2022 and found that the IRS made errors on 129 out of 133 calculations. If you were a math instructor, you would give them a grade of 3% and an F-.

Statistics reported on the IRS website at irs.gov contain a one-page summary with 129 math errors totaling $1,419,273,000,000. (See 2022 individual statistics, table 3.1)

The Internal Revenue Service doesn't have the necessary academia to operate a backyard garage sale. However, they are allowed to handle the collection and disbursement of trillions of tax dollars.

Elon Musk has barely scratched the surface regarding the efficiency of the IRS. How do the 100,000 IRS employees even begin to defend math errors totaling $1.4 trillion? This is where DOGE needs more than computer wizards. He should park a team of tax experts inside the walls of the IRS. I estimate DOGE would cut fraud between **$500 billion** and **$1 trillion**.

Internal Revenue Service

Summary of $1.4 Trillion in Math Errors

Year: 2022

DESCRIPTION	IRS CALC	CPA CALC	ERROR (in thousands)
No.of Total Returns	110,640,000	161,337,000	(50,697,000)
No. of Tax Credit Returns	43,628,000	61,832,000	(18,204,000)
Total Tax Credit Amount	$121,220,000	$154,773,000	(33,553,000)
No. of Foreign Tax Credits	10,821,000	11,310,000	(489,000)
Total Foreign Tax Amount	$30,037,000	$32,886,000	(2,849,000)
No. of Child Credit Returns	3,971,000	5,625,000	(1,654,000)
Total Child Credit Amount	$2,439,000	$3,450,000	(1,011,000)
Nonrefundable Edu Credits	4,638,000	7,528,000	(2,890,000)
Total Nonrefundable Amount	$5,115,000	$7,851,000	(2,736,000)
No. of Retirement Savings Credit	5,268,000	9,350,000	(4,082,000)
Total Retirement Credit Amount	$825,000	$1,810,000	(985,000)
No. of Nonrefundable Child Credits	25,270,000	38,295,000	(13,025,000)
Total Nonrefundable Amount	$62,825,000	$83,033,000	(20,208,000)
No of Residential Energy Credits	2,466,000	3,210,000	(744,000)
Total Residential Credit Amount	5,215,000	$8,238,000	(3,023,000)
No of Other Non Refund Returns	945,000	1,220,000	(275,000)
Total Other Nonrefundable Amount	$10,315,000	$11,275,000	(960,000)
No of General Business Credits	460,000	528,000	(68,000)
Total General Business Amount	$7,077,000	$7,384,000	(307,000)
No of Prior Min Tax Credit	105,000	114,000	(9,000)
Total Prior Min Tax Credi Amount	$1,346,000	$1,395,000	(49,000)
No of Adoprtion Credit Returns	11,000	58,000	(47,000)
Total Adoption Credit Amount	$32,000	$258,000	(226,000)
No of Credit for Elderly/Disabled	20,000	70,000	(50,000)
Total Credit for Elderly/Dis Amount	$1,000	$5,000	(4,000)
No of Fuel Vehicle Refueling Returns	20,000	42,000	(22,000)
Total Fuel Vehicle Credit Amount	$124,000	$189,000	(65,000)
No of Alternative Fuel Vehicle Returns	95,000	98,000	(3,000)
Total Alternative Fuel Credit Amounts	$40,000	$42,000	(2,000)
No of Qualified Plub-in Vehicle Returns	193,000	248,000	(55,000)
Total Qualifed Plug-in Vehicle Amount	$1,403,000	$1,652,000	(249,000)
No of Qualifed Mortgage Credit Returns	69,000	89,000	(20,000)
Total Qualfied Mortgage Credit Amount	$105,000	$140,000	(35,000)
No of Refundable Credit Returns	5,130,000	35,487,000	(30,357,000)
Total Refundable Credit Amount	$4,443,000	$112,737,000	(108,294,000)
No of Earned Income Credit Returns	1,118,000	24,086,000	(22,968,000)
Total Earned Income Credit Amount	$303,000	$60,069,000	(59,766,000)

Internal Revenue Service

Summary of $1.4 Trillion in Math Errors

Year: 2022

DESCRIPTION	IRS CALC	CPA CALC	ERROR (in thousands)
Refundable Child Tax Credit Returns	354,000	18,076,000	(17,722,000)
Total Refundable Credit Amount	$846,000	$34,843,000	(33,997,000)
No of American Opportunity Credits	2,578,000	5,957,000	(3,379,000)
Total Refundable Credit Amount	$2,086,000	$5,184,000	(3,098,000)
No of Net Premium Tax Credit	762,000	2,319,000	(1,557,000)
Total Net Premium Amount	$491,000	$2,389,000	(1,898,000)
No of Qual Sick & Family Cr Returns	14,000	436,000	(422,000)
Total Qual Sick & Family Cr Amount	$15,000	$3,217,000	(3,202,000)
No of Qual Sick & Family Cr Returns	9,000	411,000	(402,000)
Total Qual Sick & Family Cr Amount	$14,000	$3,632,000	(3,618,000)
No of Refundable Credit Offset Returns	5,129,000	7,867,000	(2,738,000)
Total Refundable Credit Amount	$4,443,000	$6,223,000	(1,780,000)
No of EIC Used to Offset Tax Ret	1,119,000	2,869,000	(1,750,000)
Total EIC Used to Offset Tax Amount	$303,000	$908,000	(605,000)
No of Refundable Child Tax Returns	354,000	513,000	(159,000)
Total Refundable Credit Amount	$845,000	$1,173,000	(328,000)
No of American Opportunity Returns	2,578,000	3,039,000	(461,000)
Total American Opportunity Cred Amt	$2,087,000	2,306,000	(219,000)
No of Income Tax Afer Credit Returns	110,612,000	110,612,000	0
Total Income Tax After Credit Amount	$2,098,923,000	2,098,923,000	0
No of Investment Income Tax Returns	7,136,000	7,141,000	(5,000)
Total Investment Income Tax Amount	$40,993,000	40,994,000	(1,000)
No of Total Income Tax Returns	110,640,000	110,640,000	0
Total of Total Income Tax Amount	$2,139,922,000	2,139,922,000	0
No of All Other Taxes Returns	24,520,000	36,666,000	(12,146,000)
Total of All Other Taxes Amount	$90,895,000	111,568,000	(20,673,000)
No of Self-Employed Tax Returns	12,389,000	22,434,000	(10,045,000)
Total Self-Employed Tax Amount	$61,838,000	81,018,000	(19,180,000)
No of So Security Taxes on Tips Ret	44,000	85,000	(41,000)
Total of So Security Taxes Tips Amount	$8,000	17,000	(9,000)
No of Uncollected So Sec Tax Returns	33,000	60,000	(27,000)
Total of Uncollected So Sec Tax Amt	$14,000	31,000	(17,000)
No of Addnl So Sec & Medicare Ret	74,000	142,000	(68,000)
Amount of Addnl So Sec & Med Amt	$22,000	48,000	(26,000)
No of Uncollected So Sec Grp Returns	505,000	606,000	(101,000)
Amount of Uncollected So Sec Grp Amt	$224,000	267,000	(43,000)

Internal Revenue Service

Summary of $1.4 Trillion in Math Errors

Year: 2022

DESCRIPTION	IRS CALC	CPA CALC	ERROR (in thousands)
No of Interest on Defered Tax Returns	9,000	10,000	(1,000)
Total of Interest on Deferred Tax Amt	$308,000	316,000	(8,000)
No of Penalty Tax on Qual Retire Ret	3,868,000	4,789,000	(921,000)
Total of Penalty Tax on Qual Ret Amt	$5,230,000	5,646,000	(416,000)
No of Household Employ Cred Returns	161,000	226,000	(65,000)
Total of Household Employ Cred Amt	$1,253,000	1,354,000	(101,000)
No of First Time Homebuyer Returns	356,000	459,000	(103,000)
Total of First Time Homebuyer Cr Amt	$178,000	227,000	(49,000)
No of Addnl Medicare Tax Returns	6,939,000	6,974,000	(35,000)
Total of Addnl Medicare Tax Amount	$15,038,000	15,087,000	(49,000)
No of Addnl Taxes Returns	330,000	372,000	(42,000)
Total of Addnl Taxes Returns	$495,000	519,000	(24,000)
No of Refund Cred Offset Other Ret	0	8,914,000	(8,914,000)
Total of Refund Cred Offset Other Amt	$0	12,297,000	(12,297,000)
No of EIC Used to Offset Tax Ret	0	7,087,000	(7,087,000)
Total of EIC Used to Offset Tax Amt	$0	8,848,000	(8,848,000)
No of Refund Cred Offset Other Ret	0	1,643,000	(1,643,000)
Total of Refund Cred Offset Other Amt	$0	2,291,000	(2,291,000)
No of American Opportunity Off Ret	0	413,000	(413,000)
Total American Opportunity Cred Amt	0	207,000	(207,000)
No of Tax Liability Returns	110,640,000	116,295,000	(5,655,000)
Total of Tax Liability Amounts	$2,230,637,000	2,238,645,000	(8,008,000)
No of Returns w Tax Payments	107,205,000	141,173,000	(33,968,000)
Total Tax Withheld	$2,304,182,000	2,365,775,000	(61,593,000)
No of Income Tax w/h Returns	104,784,000	137,846,000	(33,062,000)
Total of Income Tax w/h Amount	$1,517,983,000	1,566,743,000	(48,760,000)
No of W-2's with Income Tax w/h	91,069,000	120,464,000	(29,395,000)
Total Income Tax w/h on W-2's	$1,322,372,000	1,363,255,000	(40,883,000)
No of 1099's with Income Tax w/h	27,084,000	32,364,000	(5,280,000)
Total Income Tax w/h on 1099's	$175,450,000	182,760,000	(7,310,000)
No of Other Forms with Income Tax w/h	6,083,000	6,282,000	(199,000)
Total Income Tax w/h Other Forms	$16,514,000	16,933,000	(419,000)
No of Returns w/ Estimated Tax Pymts	9,577,000	10,534,000	(957,000)
Total Income Tax Estimated Pymts	$572,644,000	581,222,000	(8,578,000)
No of Returns w/ Req for Extension	1,948,000	2,094,000	(146,000)
Total Income Tax Paid w/ Extension	$202,742,000	203,886,000	(1,144,000)
No of Returns w/ Excess So Sec	2,099,000	2,123,000	(24,000)
Total Excess So Sec Amount	$5,830,000	5,859,000	(29,000)

Internal Revenue Service

Summary of $1.4 Trillion in Math Errors

Year: 2022

DESCRIPTION	IRS CALC	CPA CALC	ERROR (in thousands)
No of Returns w/ Fed Tax on Gasoline	243,000	569,000	(326,000)
Total Fed Tax on Gasoline Amount	$4,421,000	7,188,000	(2,767,000)
No of Returns w/ Refundable Credits	0	27,444,000	(27,444,000)
Total Refundable Credit Amount	$0	94,218,000	(94,218,000)
No of EIC Refundable Credit Returns	0	20,525,000	(20,525,000)
Total EIC Refundable Credit Amount	$0	50,312,000	(50,312,000)
No of Returns w/ Child Tax Cr	0	16,746,000	(16,746,000)
Total Child Tax Credit Amount	$0	31,379,000	(31,379,000)
No of American Opportunity Returns	0	3,174,000	(3,174,000)
Total American Opportunity Cred Amt	$0	2,672,000	(2,672,000)
No of Returns w/ Tax & Refund Credits	110,640,000	141,252,000	(30,612,000)
Total Tax & Refund Credits Amount	$2,139,922,000	2,033,060,000	106,862,000
No of Returns w/ Tax Overpayment	72,705,000	112,860,000	(40,155,000)
Total Tax Overpayment Amounts	$347,970,000	501,047,000	(153,077,000)
No of Returns w/ Refunds	69,701,000	109,581,000	(39,880,000)
Total Returns w/ Refunds Amount	$218,229,000	367,538,000	(149,309,000)
No of Returns w/ Est Tax Pymts	3,975,000	4,402,000	(427,000)
Total Returns w/ Est Tax Pymts Amount	$129,740,000	133,509,000	(3,769,000)
No of Returns w/ Tax Due	37,664,000	41,855,000	(4,191,000)
Total Returns w/ Tax Due Amount	$278,680,000	284,147,000	(5,467,000)
No of Returns w/ Tax Penalties	13,088,000	14,072,000	(984,000)
Total Returns w/ Tax Penalties Amount	$4,047,000	4,126,000	(79,000)
	17,464,585,000	**18,883,858,000**	**(1,419,273,000)**

Chapter 13: IRS Giving Millions to Criminals & Terrorists

The combination of outdated technology and equipment resulted in the IRS processing **2.6 million** tax fraud refunds during the COVID-19 pandemic.

- **24,000 Refunds to Single Mailbox**
- **Cocaine Dealers Now Tax Frauds**
- **Sale of 10,000 Computers to Iran**
- **Al Qaeda Members Based in Iran**

According to the Small Business Administration, one-third of small businesses permanently closed during the pandemic.

IRS statistics show that in 2019, 5.4 million self-employed businesses received the Earned Income Tax Credit. The SBA estimated that 1.8 million (33% x 5.4 million) of those businesses permanently closed in 2020. Therefore, if you take the pre-pandemic businesses of 5.4 million and subtract closings of 1.8 million, you arrive at a total of 3.6 million post-pandemic businesses at the end of 2020. In contrast, the IRS indicated that **profitable** small businesses qualifying for an Earned Income Credit rose to **6.2 million**.

Description	**2019 (000's)**	**2020 (000's)**	**2020 S/E EITC Frauds**
SE EITC Refunds	5,400	6,200	
Less: Business Closings 33%	(1,800)		
Expected 2020 SE Refunds		(3,600)	**2,600**

During the **worst economic period** in the last 70 years, why would parents with **no money** decide to start businesses? The answer is that **it never happened**. The average small business saw revenues and profits drop by **50%**.

Nina Olson, formerly in charge of the Taxpayer Advocate Office, stated that the IRS doesn't check their calculations for accuracy.

Senator Bill Nelson of the Finance Sub-Committee on Fiscal Responsibility and Economic Growth addressed the issue of earned income credit fraud: "We're here today to talk about a serious crime that a South Florida federal prosecutor recently described as an epidemic. People describe it as **cocaine on a card**."

24,000 Tax Refunds to a Single Mailbox

Forest Gump memorialized the line, "I'm not a smart man." I think it's safe to say that even Forest Gump would agree that issuing 23,994 tax refunds totaling $46 million to the same mailbox is pretty stupid. Treasury Inspector General for Tax Administration Russell George was quoted as saying, "This is one of those rare cases when we actually validated almost every allegation that was alleged."

The TIGTA audit revealed that the perpetrators were undocumented workers who utilized the same address for multiple filings. In some instances, the illegal immigrants claimed up to ten nieces and nephews as dependents on their taxes. The problem was that they didn't reside in the United States.

Criminals have migrated from selling drugs to stealing identities to obtain tax refunds from the IRS. Why would someone want to risk prison when you can steal money from the IRS and risk a minimal chance of going to jail?

Steve Kroft of **60 Minutes** interviewed a tax fraud sitting by his pool. One morning, he submitted fraudulent returns seeking $25,000.

He boasted that his success rate was 30%. This means the fraudster made a cool $7,500 for 4 hours of work. This epidemic isn't limited to Atlanta. According to the Treasury Inspector, six other cities made their list. (See below)

Location	**Refunds to 1 Mailbox**	**Tax Fraud**
Atlanta, GA	23,994	$46.4 Mil
Atlanta, GA	11,284	$2.2 Mil
Atlanta, GA	3,608	$2.7 Mil
Atlanta, GA	2,386	$1.2 Mil
Oxnard, CA	2,507	$10.4 Mil
Raleigh, NC	2,408	$7.3 Mil
Phoenix, AZ	2,047	$5.6 Mil
Palm Beach, FL	1,972	$2.3 Mil
San Jose, CA	1,942	$5.1 Mil
Arvin, CA	1,846	$3.3 Mil
Totals	**53,994**	**$86.5 Mil**

(Figure 14.1 Treasury Inspector General)

We can agree that sending 54,000 checks to 10 addresses personifies the extreme level of dysfunction inside the walls for the IRS.

One month after the TIGTA report was released, I contacted the IRS to present an AI technology I had developed called **Earned Income Credit Compliance Audit (EICCA)**. I proposed testing 6.5 million tax returns to detect fraudulent claims and potentially save the US Treasury billions of dollars.

The IRS dissected my proposal and called to express high interest. Three months later, the IRS returned my proposal, saying that they already had a prototype of my software (why did they call me in the first place?) and that they didn't have any money to pay me anyway.

Following the **Tea Party Congressional Hearings**, I learned that the IRS had entered into a $500 million software agreement with Strong Castle, a company connected to a personal acquaintance of an IRS employee, exactly three months after I submitted my proposal. This revelation exposed a serious discrepancy in the IRS's actions. I had caught them in a horrible lie.

10,000 Computers Sold to Iran

The US Attorney's Office in the Dallas, TX Division indicted Borna Faizy and Roura Ghavided for plotting to send $12 million worth of computers to Iran. The indictment alleges that Faizy and Ghavided acquired computers from US companies to supply to end-users in Iran and concealed from the United States that the computers were destined for Iran.

Dallas-Area Businessmen Charged in Plot Involving Illegal Export of Approximately $12 Million Worth of Computers to Iran

Defendants Allegedly Shipped Computers to Dubai, Concealing That They were Ultimately Destined for Iran

U.S. Attorney's Office — **Northern District of Texas**
March 08, 2013 — (214) 659-8600

(http://www.fbi.gov/dallas/press-releases/2013/dallas-area-businessmen-charged-in-plot-involving-illegal-export-of-approximately-12-million-worth-of-computers-to-iran8

In a similar scheme one year earlier, the U.S. Department of Justice thwarted the efforts of Massoud Habibion and Mohsen Motamedian for attempting to export $5 million in computer equipment to Iran.

In 2012, US District Judge Ellen S. Huvelle sentenced the pair. As part of their guilty pleas, Habibion agreed to forfeit $1.9 million seized by Homeland Security Investigations.

Department of Justice
Office of Public Affairs

Two Individuals and Their California Company Sentenced in Connection with Exports of Computer Equipment

Massoud Habibion, 49, a U.S. citizen, Mohsen Motamedian, 44, a U.S. citizen, and their Costa Mesa, Calif., company, Online Micro LLC,

(http://www.justice.gov/opa/pr/2012/May/12-nsd-629.html)

In 2007, Habibion's company, Online Micro, purchased 1,000 computers from Dell for approximately $500,000. Later that year, Dell began receiving service calls related to those units originating from an unexpected location: Iran.

Clearly, the pair should have insisted on a signed NDA (Non-Disclosure Agreement). This is the same year the Great Recession started, and the IRS failed to detect 3 million new tax frauds.

I've never taken a class on the Ethics of a Terrorist. But I'm guessing if lopping the head off a foreign journalist is OK then sitting poolside filing fraudulent tax returns wouldn't be problematic.

Leading Al Qaeda Members are based in Iran

CNN reported that the 9/11 Commission found that, of the 19 hijackers, "8 to 10 of the 14 Saudi muscle operatives" traveled to or from Iran between October 2000 and February 2001. According to journalist Peter Bergen, Iran has served as a haven for Al Qaeda for more than a decade.

TIGTA: Billions of Dollars in Tax Refund Theft Go Undetected

In August 2012, the **Treasury Inspector General for Tax Administration** issued an audit report stating that the impact of identity theft on tax administration is significantly greater than what the **Internal Revenue Service** is able to detect.

Description	**Returns**	**Stopped**	**Fraud**
Detected Fraud	940,000	$6.5 Bil	
Undetected	1,500,000		$5.2 Bil
TIGTA Projected Fraud - 4 Years			**$21 Bil**

(https://www.treasury.gov/tigta/press/press_tigta-2012-36.htm)

Potential Terrorist Tax Refund Fraud	
Treasury General Projected Tax Fraud	$21 Bil
Est. Terrorist Refunds for Every 100 Frauds	1.0%
Est. Cash Paid to Terrorists	**$210,000,000**

The internet shows the average cost of an IED (Improvised Explosive Device) $500

Est. Cash Paid to Terrorists	$210,000,000
Divided by IED Cost	$500
IED Potential Purchases	420,000

Iraq Weapon of Most Destruction

In a guest column for **The Washington Post**, Army Lt. Gen. Michael Barbero reported that during the first decade of combat operations in Iraq and Afghanistan, improvised explosive devices were the weapon of choice for threat networks.

IEDs are makeshift weapons that incorporate destructive, lethal chemicals, military-grade or commercially available explosives, or homemade explosive materials. The components used to assemble IEDs are inexpensive and readily available at hardware stores. Lt. General Barbero also noted that the use of IEDs extends beyond conflict zones, citing the **Boston Marathon bombing** as a notable example.

He provided statistics that showed **60%** of US combat casualties in Iraq and Afghanistan stemmed from IEDs. The table below shows the impact of IEDs:

Iraq/Afghanistan Conflict	U.S. Troops	60% Casualties from IED
Killed	3,200	1,900
Wounded	33,100	19,900
Total	35,300	21,800

)https://www.washingtonpost.com/opinions/improvised-explosive-devices-are-here-to- stay/2013/05/17/8d9c9d7c-be64-11e2-9b09-1638acc3942e_story.html

Lt. General Barbero stated that money is the lifeblood of these networks, so we must attack them where it hurts the most, their **bank accounts**. He opined our current approach is disjointed with too many organizations doing too little.

Ease of Transfer – Refund Debit Cards

If you’re a terrorist without a bank account, you can request your refund on a debit card. The above box has the capacity of 640 refund cards. Based on the average tax refund of $5,000, that represents a box containing $3,200,000.

Black Friday Shopping & 14 Day Refunds

Back in 1980, when you filed your tax return, it wasn't unusual to wait 8 weeks before receiving a refund. In the last 40 years, technology has propelled us into a microwave society. We want to be fed quickly, paid quickly and prefer texting to making a phone call. The IRS followed suit by shortening the wait time on tax refunds from 50-70 to 10-14 days.

The problem is that IRS technology is antiquated. Therefore, the verification of W-2 and 1099 tax information isn't timely.

Black Friday used to be a reward for early risers with long shopping lists. Now, it's turned into total chaos, with impatient shoppers pushing and fighting.

Historically, retailers have relied on the holiday season for as much as 25% of their annual sales. While the shopping frenzy may bring joy to many, it also puts a hefty amount of pressure on parents, who are well aware that a huge credit card bill will arrive in January.

IRS statistics show that as many as 40 million taxpayers will receive their tax refunds by March 15th. The IRS doesn't put out any data regarding how many Black Friday shoppers receive early tax refunds, but conservatively, it must be in the millions.

Lt. General Babero believes that the threat networks utilizing IEDs will remain in the future.

Question:

Why does getting money in the pockets of holiday shoppers take precedence over safeguarding American troops and citizens?

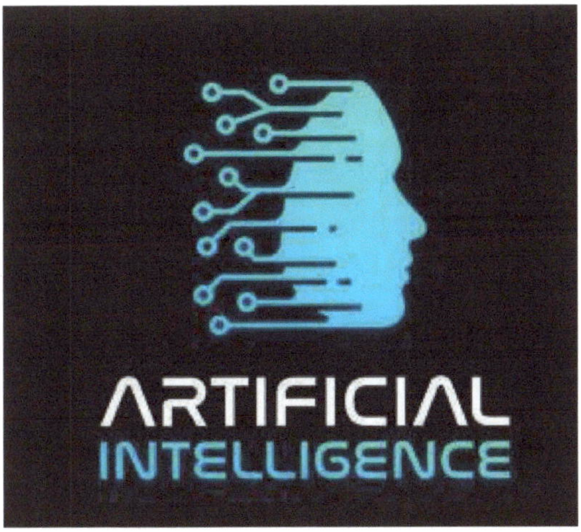

Chapter 14: AI Can Identify 6 Mil Tax Frauds 1 Day

The Treasury Inspector General for Tax Administration estimates that the IRS loses up to $16 billion annually due to fraudulent claims for the Earned Income Tax Credits. I have developed AI technology capable of analyzing 30 million EITC tax returns in a single day.

A common trait of tax fraudsters is greed. It is similar to a parishioner taking money from the offering plate. Rather than taking one or five dollars, they take ten. The same mentality applies to tax fraud. The theme seems to be go big or go home. My company previously tested 535,000 tax returns containing 80 fields of tax data in just 45 minutes. Our findings show that the IRS is being defrauded in three primary ways: taxpayers reporting phantom income, individuals deducting fictitious expenses, and the submission of fake W-2 forms.

AI tech identifies tax filers who report gross income in even $100 increments. By utilizing a set of proprietary algorithms, we will identify one million EITC recipients who claim phantom income and expenses. Once a person is identified, they will receive an email indicating they have been selected to participate in the Earned Income Credit Compliance Audit. No scare tactics are required.

The individual will be required to visit a link at irs.gov and input their monthly gross revenue. If the total revenue is close to the same, they pass the audit and can expect their refund in the next 10 to 14 days. However, if they're unable to enter accurate amounts of revenue, then their credit will be denied. Appeals can be immediately filed with additional supporting business records.

The third group of tax fraudsters is estimated to include approximately 5 million individuals who report nonexistent W-2 data. Many people are skeptical when I raise this issue, but the truth is that the IRS does a poor job of cross-checking tax return data against the **actual wage information** reported to the Social Security Administration.

When I brought this issue to the attention of the IRS, they initially dismissed it. I even contacted the individual responsible for that department, who assured me such a scenario was not possible. He was wrong. One of my tax clients became a victim of fraud when an imposter filed a false tax return claiming $22,500 in federal tax withholding. The correct amount was $0. The IRS processed the return and issued a check for $7,500.

Although employers are required to provide W-2s to employees by January 31st, outdated technology from the 1990s prevents the IRS from verifying reported wages in real time. I estimate that the US Treasury would save up to $100 billion by verifying income and tax withholding **prior** to issuing refunds.

DOGE should mandate that the IRS verify ALL federal tax deposits before releasing any refunds. This is a matter of common sense and fiscal responsibility.

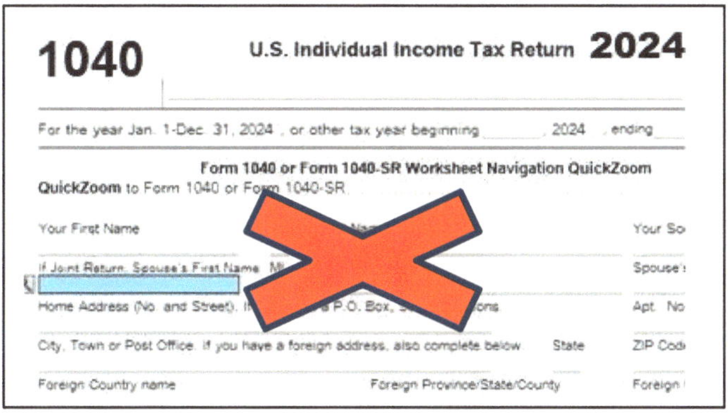

Chapter 15: Eliminate Tax Filing for 120 Million

President Trump announced that he wants to abolish the IRS and replace it with tariffs. I performed a deep dive on personal income taxes and determined that tax filing could be abolished for 120 million taxpayers earning $100,000 or less. This would only result in a 10% decline in revenue to the US Treasury.

DOGE has succeeded in cutting government waste and improving efficiency. Congress needs to change the tax code to require only those earning over $100,000 to file tax returns.

A Verification of Annual Income would replace IRS Form 1040 for individuals earning $100,000 or less. Everyone would be extended the option to file to continue receiving tax credits such as earned income tax credits or healthcare subsidies. A more streamlined option would be to have the IRS automatically calculate the refundable tax credits.

Self-employed individuals would pay social security taxes based on reported annual income. Social security taxes would be calculated in **real time.** People would still be subject to being **audited** to ensure compliance. The penalty for non-compliance would be 100% of taxes on actual income or $5,000, whichever is greater.

It is clear the lion's share of taxes are paid by taxpayers earning over $100,000. According to statistics on the IRS.gov website, this group comprises approximately 40 million taxpayers and is responsible for 86% of all income tax revenue.

Adj Gross Income	Taxpayers	Amount	%
$0 to $100,000	120 Mil	$310 Bil	14%
$100,001 plus	40 Mil	$1,930 Bil	86%
Total	**160 Mil**	**$2,340 Bil**	**100%**

Since the Great Recession, Americans have become lax in paying their income taxes by April 15th. In addition, tax fraud from identity theft has risen exponentially in the last 10 years.

I believe experts would concede that the group of 120 million taxpayers is probably responsible for $100 billion in tax fraud. Below is a breakdown between the income tax liability, unpaid taxes, cost of fraud and net taxes collected on April 15th.

Description	Taxpayers	Amount
Income Tax Liability	120 Mil	$310 Bil
Unpaid Taxes @ Filing	24 Mil	(40 Bil)
Subtotal		$270 Bil
Less: Cost of Fraud	120 Mil	(100 Bil)
Net Taxes Collected	**120 Mil**	**$170 Bil**

When unpaid taxes and fraud are considered, the 120 million taxpayers are responsible for **8%** of personal tax revenue collected by the U.S. Treasury.

If the IRS receives 90% fewer tax returns, it's common sense that the budget and workforce could be proportionately reduced.

The timing of modifying the tax filing requirement will align with the potential retirement of a large portion of the IRS workforce. The number of IRS employees eligible for retirement during the next two years is significant.

Abolishing the IRS isn't a perfect solution. However, the dialogue must begin to address the elephant in the room.

Chapter 16: How to Win $6 Million

How would you like to be a silent whistleblower? How does it work? I need to obtain tax statistics that the Internal Revenue Service won't release.

Here's where you come in. If you can obtain the tax information on the next page, I will pay you $6 million. There are two conditions. First, I can only pay you with the proceeds from a Whistleblower

Office reward. Two, you need to provide the tax statistics before I secure the data. You will be considered to have **met this condition** if a new whistleblower claim hasn't been filed before your submission. If I recover less than $6 million, you will receive 100% of any reward money I receive. I'm not interested in getting rich, but I want to know the truth.

Description	Year	Amount
Fed tax w/h on Social Security	2018	$1,608
Fed tax w/h on Social Security	2019	$1,626
Fed tax w/h on Social Security	2020	$1,735
Fed tax w/h on Social Security	2021	$1,782
Fed tax w/h on Social Security	2022	$2,041
Fed tax w/h on Social Security	2023	$1,979

Your job is to find out the number of federal returns that reported federal tax withholding from their Social Security Benefits in 2018 for $1,608, the number of returns that filed federal tax withholding in 2019 that listed $1,626, and the same for years 2020 through 2023.

I submitted a whistleblower claim last July that the IRS rejected after only one week. I proposed recovering **$200 million** on behalf of taxpayers. A prominent national tax software company was notified in June 2020 that their clients were receiving money that didn't belong to them.

Based on their willingness to let their clients defraud the Internal Revenue Service, they are liable for between $20 and $200 million that was falsely paid to their clients. Over five years, this represents between **$100 million** and **$1 billion** in recoverable money for the US Treasury.

My contact information is listed below if you strike gold by securing the tax information:

Randall C Sorensen CPA
7150 E Camelback Rd. Ste 444
Scottsdale, AZ 85251
Ph: 480.344.2970

Email: Randall.C.Sorensen@gmail.com

Chapter 17: Abolish IRS in Favor of National Sales Tax

The time has come for Congress to phase out the Internal Revenue Service. Since nearly half of the agency's workforce can retire in less than five years, the agency won't have the staff to operate efficiently.

You can't abolish the IRS overnight. The first step would be to require only individuals earning over $100,000 to file. This would keep revenue at 90%.

A Verification of Annual Income would replace IRS Form 1040. Individuals earning less than $100,001 could still continue filing to receive tax credits like the earned income and healthcare tax credits.

The second step is to secure an alternative revenue source for the US Treasury. I propose a national sales tax between 12% and 15%. You would want to test this for one year to confirm its viability. This would accomplish five things:

1. Everyone would pay their **fair share**
2. Reduce required IRS employees by **90,000**
3. Remove **$100** billion in tax fraud
4. Slash into the **$300** billion tax gap
5. Provide **peace of mind** to Americans, knowing the IRS was no longer in the business of funding terrorists.

If Congress needs proof of the IRS funding terrorists, then give me 24-hour access to the tax refund database.

Diagnostic tests would be conducted to identify individuals who have received three or more tax refunds. These recipient names would then be cross-checked against international air bills processed by the U.S. Postal Service, FedEx, UPS, and other carriers operating in Europe and the Middle East.

Congress would receive a list of potential terrorist sympathizers in less than a fortnight that would justify abolishing the IRS due to security reasons.

If you support abolishing the IRS, please send an email to Randall.C.Sorensen@gmail.com.

Thank you.